Crossing to Sunlight

Crossing to Sunlight

SELECTED POEMS BY

Paul Zimmer

The University of Georgia Press

Athens & London

Published by the

University of Georgia Press

Athens, Georgia 30602

© 1996 by Paul Zimmer

Designed by Richard Hendel

Set in Monotype Garamond by Books International

Printed and bound by Thomson-Shore

Photographic image from an autochrome

by Heinrich Kühn.

The paper in this book meets the guidelines

for permanence and durability of the Committee on

Production Guidelines for Book Longevity of the

Council on Library Resources.

Printed in the United States of America

oo 99 98 97 96 c 5 4 3 2 1

oo 99 98 97 96 p 5 4 3 2 1

Library of Congress Cataloging in Publication Data

Zimmer, Paul.

    Crossing to sunlight : selected poems / Paul Zimmer.

      p. cm.

    ISBN 0-8203-1818-3 (alk. paper). —ISBN 0-8203-1829-9 (pbk. :

alk. paper)

      I. Title

PS3576.147A6   1996

811'.54—dc20   95-43435

British Library Cataloging in Publication Data available

TO SUZANNE

my one and only love

TO ERIK & JUSTINE

ACKNOWLEDGMENTS

The author and publisher wish to thank the following publishers for permission to reprint poems from the following volumes: *The Ribs of Death* (1967) and *The Republic of Many Voices* (1969), October House; *The Zimmer Poems* (1976) and *With Wanda: Town and Country Poems* (1980), Dryad Press; *Family Reunion: Selected and New Poems* (1983), University of Pittsburgh Press; *The Great Bird of Love* (1989), University of Illinois Press; *Big Blue Train* (1993), University of Arkansas Press. Some of the poems appear in slightly altered forms.

The author and publisher gratefully acknowledge the following journals in which some poems originally appeared.

Doubletake: "Crossing to Sunlight"

Georgia Review: "The Books" and "Before the Moon Came Up Last Night"

Gettysburg Review: "The Example," "Dear Mom," "Grouse," and "Suck It Up"

Iowa Review: "In Apple Country" and "The End before the End"

Laurel Review: "Love Poem" and "Blood Lock"

Plum Review: "And Then I Drove On"

Tar River Review: "Divestment," "Pearl-Handled Pistols," and

"The Poetry of Aging Men"

Contents

Crossing to Sunlight *1*
from *The Ribs of Death* (1967)
Apple Blight *5*
Handel's Music for the Royal Fireworks *6*
Two Studies of Mary Dodd *7*
Lord Fluting Dreams of America on the
Eve of His Departure from Liverpool *10*

from *The Republic of Many Voices* (1969)
Julian Dreams of Being under All Trees *13*
Willis in the Rise and Fall of Trainscape *14*
Thurman Dreaming in Right Field *15*
Zimmer's Head Thudding against the Blackboard *16*
Zimmer Guilty of the Burnt Girl *17*
Zimmer and His Turtle Sink the House *18*
Entering the Storm, Unable to Swim, Zimmer,
Rollo, and Cecil Are Saved *19*
Zimmer Drunk and Alone, Dreaming of
Old Football Games *20*
Zimmer's Love Poem after a Hard Dream *21*

from *The Zimmer Poems* (1976)
Zimmer in Grade School *25*
What Zimmer Would Be *26*
One for the Ladies at the Troy Laundry Who Cooled
Themselves for Zimmer *28*
Father Animus and Zimmer *29*
The Sweet Night Bleeds from Zimmer *31*
Cecil, Zimmer, and the Man-Made Lake *33*
A Zimmershire Lad *35*
Zumer Is Icumen In *36*
The Day Zimmer Lost Religion *37*

Zimmer the Drugstore Cowboy *38*
Leaves of Zimmer *40*
An Enzyme Poem for Suzanne *41*
Zimmer Envying Elephants *42*
Zimmer Loathing the Gentry *43*
Death Demonstrates His Presence to Zimmer *44*
Zimmer's Bed *45*

from *With Wanda: Town and Country Poems* (1980)
Wanda Being Beautiful *49*
Wanda and the Fish *50*
Wanda Dreams of Eli and the Farm *51*
Rollo's Miracle *53*
Robyn Hode and Maid Wanda *54*
Lester Tells of Wanda and the Big Snow *55*
Lester Tells of the End of Summer *56*
Dear Wanda (Letter from Rollo) *57*
Dear Wanda (Letter from Zimmer) *58*
Gus in the Streets *59*
Thurman's Slumping Blues *60*
Zimmer's Last Gig *61*
Dear Wanda (Letter from Christiaan) *63*
Gus Sees Wanda Drinking *64*
Dear Wanda (Letter from Cecil) *66*
Zimmer and the Ghost *67*

from *Family Reunion* (1983)
Once as a Child I Had Bad Dreams *71*
Irene Gogle *72*
The Eisenhower Years *73*
The Ancient Wars *75*
The Duke Ellington Dream *77*
The Great House *78*
A Final Affection *79*

When Angels Came to Zimmer *80*
Work *81*
Zimmer Imagines Heaven *83*

from *The Great Bird of Love* (1989)
The Dream of My Second Conscription *87*
The Origins of Love *88*
Two Drinking Songs *89*
The Poets' Strike *91*
Lessons from the History of Bears *92*
The Sounds of Magpie *94*
The Old Trains at Night *95*
How Zimmer Will Be Reborn *97*
Yellow Sonnet *99*
Sitting with Lester Young *100*
The Tenth Circle *101*
The Explanation *102*
Winter *103*
The Place *104*
The Great Bird of Love *105*

from *Big Blue Train* (1993)
The Persistence of Fatherhood *109*
Fog in the Valley *110*
What I Know about Owls *111*
A Romance for the Wild Turkey *112*
The Brain of the Spider *113*
But Bird *114*
The Light *116*
Diz's Face *118*
Romance *120*
The Existential Year *121*
The Beautiful Ethiopian Navy *122*
The Weathers of Love *124*

A Rant against Losses *126*
Raw and Absolute *127*
The Seed Bearers *128*
Another Place *130*
Big Blue Train *131*

New Poems
  Entrance to the Sky *135*
  The Books *140*
  Knee-Deep in Wildflowers *142*
  Love Poem *143*
  Grouse *144*
  Before the Moon Came Up Last Night *145*
  Divestment *146*
  The Poetry of Aging Men *147*
  Greatness *148*
  Milkweed *149*
  The Name for Money *151*
  The Example *152*
  Suck It Up *153*
  Dear Mom *155*
  Passage *157*
  And Then I Drove On *158*
  Blood Lock *159*
  Pearl-Handled Pistols *161*
  As I Walked the Road *163*
  The End before the End *164*
  In Apple Country *165*

Crossing to Sunlight

Crossing to Sunlight

The old road through woods is
Like a vein of my slow blood.
To walk it with reflection
Is like being cured of a malady.
I need nothing more than this
Amble through checkered light
Under big trees and saplings crossing,
Down to the ravine, then rising
To the two lobes of meadows
Stretched across the ridge,
One slanted in shadow light
The other tilted to full sun.
I ramble from yin to yang,
To where light holds morning,
Brushing it through the grass.
Crickets stop at my footfalls,
Birds cease skimming the tufts,
Then everything begins once more—
What was dull now shines,
What was silent is defined.
I have risen to sunlight where
The dimming must begin again.

from

The Ribs of Death (1967)

"I was all ear,
And took in strains that might create a soul
Under the ribs of death . . ."

John Milton, *Comus*

Apple Blight

Blighted apples will not shine.
Though they are buffed by winds
As diligent as Caesar's valets,
The fog has settled in their skins.

Branches bow down low to death,
Dragged by blighted apples.
Cold leaves curl about the wind,
Strangled by dull apples.

Though apples host the cruelest worms,
The hardest beetles, still they shine,
But when the sickness sweeps the tree
They will not shine, they will not shine.

Handel's Music for the Royal Fireworks

Though gout was twisting at my old age,
Sixteen yards of Green Park wall were moved
To let my public in. And though opacities
Were folding in my eyes, I brought all London
Down to hear my Bourrée and my Minuets.
Then between La Paix and Rejouissance
Old Servandoni touched his punk against the fuse
And pushed the night back up into the sky.

Gog's heart! Never have I seen such
Fuming, cracking, pouring, as if the sun
Had fired a rain of oil. It bent
My quarter notes like wire and hammered
My arpeggi until they came out straighter
Than tenuto notes. We played on
Though Roman candles spit as if the war
Had come again, but when the Temple of the Peace
Began to burn as though it were the paper
Of the treaty, the music stopped abruptio.

Down Piccadilly, Pall Mall, and St. James
We ran like infantry before a Prussian volley.
And I, my new wig burning with my suite,
My old joints grinding with each stride,
Recalled the day I played my music on water,
And deemed it far safer than fire.

Two Studies of Mary Dodd

I : THE MAN

Yes sir, I remember Mary Dodd,
As wicked as a jay bird, and enough
To prickle hair out of your chest.
She was cut out of the cheesy stuff

That sets a hound to straining
At the moon, and once a week
At dawn, when dark slid down
The hills to gather in the creek,

She muttered into town for food,
Colder than the bottom of a stone.
She shuffled in her boots when there
Was not a drop to chill her bones,

And someone claimed the puddles foamed
Before she stirred them with her skirts.
Her son and husband, gone for years,
Had wrinkled with the town dirt,

And left her with a string of grief
To strum her lonely mind upon.
So struck, she tasseled every fence
Post with a can to scoop the sun.

Dead now for thirty years, her cabin
Swallowed by a swell of green,
I recall the day she died, battered
To her dirty knees by men so lean

They thought they could smell money
In the must that netted up her wall.
And now she's gone these years, except
For some like me who can recall

How cold her body was to fingers of
A boy who had gone out an afternoon
To taunt old Mary Dodd to death,
And found her lying dead too soon.

II : THE BOY

Oh Jesus, Mary Dodd is murdered,
Her skull as red as any matted rose!
I found her lying like a pile of clay
Beneath "Stay Out" signs she'd chalked
Upon her walls. Someone has thumped
The blood out of her veins!
                                        I crept up
To pelt her cabin with new apples,
And there she was, eyelids horny
As old turtle shells, cheeks as green
As apples I had dropped. The blood
Had run its petals down her head,
Her teeth were dead as yellow leaves.

As I turned to run the sun was smearing
On cans she'd tacked to fence posts,
And in the woods some starving bird
Was shrieking with its hunger.
                                        Oh Jesus,
I have been so scared at night I thought

The moon was raining bats, but Mary Dodd,
So green in sun, has made the daylight
Dark with fear.

Lord Fluting Dreams of America on the Eve of His Departure from Liverpool

Purple Indians pas de cheval
Around a Chippendale totem pole.
The Ute dips to the Crow,
And curtsies to the Navajo,
While the forest in its wig and stole
Claps its leaves politely.

Cotton and tobacco plants cluster
On the backland hills like
Plaster on a Spanish cloister.
All rivers and bright lakes are
Filled with plumed bass
Browsing on watercress.

The sylvan trail to Oregon
Is thronged with gentle post chaise
Gliding toward great fortune;
For this is where buffalo turn
Broadside to the hunting horns,
And gold is strained
Like sunshine through heath.

from

The Republic of
Many Voices (1969)

Julian Dreams of Being under All Trees

With snow spilling from jack pine cones
And sorting through the needles,
I longed for warmer trees,
For sycamores, sweetgums, aspens.
I imagined how certain and right
It would be to see them
Shift and change above my head.
I dreamt I always walked beneath maples,
Willows, hickories, butternuts, and elms.
It was all ancient, known and good,
Absolute beyond all things I dreamt.
I was cro-magnon thudding below palms,
Amoeba budding beneath groups of tiny hydra,
A comet spurting under canopies of throbbing planets.
I was Julian walking beneath jack pines in the snow.

Willis in the Rise and Fall of Trainscape

The train came timber by timber,
choking around the bend
and rhyming with dismal rain.
I did not look up
from my fire
as it came grinding,
adding to my misery.
It honked and my whiskers
wavered like cilia,
then it passed on,
offering nothing to the leaden day.
My fire collapsed and sprang
within the poor light,
then suddenly the flame dimmed,
as the sun broke like an egg
through the clouds;
and the landscape was rising,
rising as the train
blared joyously beyond me!
I stepped back and stretched
my arms toward the new sun,
but it was swallowed
by the heavy day again.
I walked back to my brightening fire
and heard the train
complaining in the distance,
rhyming with the rain again.

Thurman Dreaming in Right Field

In right field I am so far out
The batter has unwound before
I hear the crack of his effort,
And the ball whirrs out and bounces
Like wind off the wall
At idiot angles.
              I am lonely
In that distance.
                  The moon shines
Like a long fly in right field
Where rain falls first
And snow drifts in winter.
Sun cuts intricate shadows from
The decks above my head
And balls, dropping like duck hawks,
Suddenly grow dull in the broken light
Of right field.
              But there is
Always time for dreaming before
The impossible catch, the wheel
And shotgun throw on one bounce to
The plate, where the catcher slams
The ball onto the sliding runner's thigh,
And the crowd goes roaring, "Thurman!"
In that far field where
I am dreaming once again.

Zimmer's Head Thudding against the Blackboard

At the blackboard I had missed
Five number problems in a row,
And was about to foul a sixth,
When the old, exasperated nun
Began to pound my head against
My six mistakes. When I cried
She threw me back into my seat,
Where I hid my head and swore
That very day I'd be a poet,
And curse her yellow teeth with this.

Zimmer Guilty of the Burnt Girl

Once a week
The burnt girl came peddling to our house,
Touching her sweet rolls with raisin fingers,
Her raw face struggling like a bubble
Through lava to say what she had
To sell and why, "Please buy my sweets
To mend my face."

Always I hid behind the piano and heard
My unflinching mother quietly buy a few,
And imagined apricots shriveling in sun,
Spiders boiling and dripping above matches.
Always when the burnt girl had gone,
I heard my mother drop her purchase
In the rubbish to be burned and
I came out to see the pink graftings,
The horrid, sugared layers of the rolls.

I do not want
The burnt girl to come again.
I am guilty for her and of her.
Always in fever I think of that face.
Sometimes in love I believe that I am fire
Consuming myself, and the burnt girl
Suffers from my love as she sells
Her rolls to mend her face.

Zimmer and His Turtle Sink the House

I had soaked the old house
Until plaster bulged like fungus
From its lath. Bead firms grew
In the rainbow spray of waterfalls
Down the carpeted stairs,
And the cellar meter clicked
Off the waters of my mistake.

I had forgotten, gone away and left
My turtle burping through water
Running in the upstairs sink,
Gone away and left the old house
Torpedoed and filling, with only
A cold-blooded helmsman on the bridge.

All the towels, old underwear, and mops
That I could muster never dried
The house up, never turned
The meter back from what it told.

The turtle was gone.
Swept to the basement no doubt
Where it had grown into a loggerhead,
Grumbling and steel-jawed like my father,
Angry at my carelessness, ready to snap
My digits off if I gave him
Half a chance.

Entering the Storm, Unable to Swim, Zimmer, Rollo, and Cecil Are Saved

A storm mixed and fell upon the lake
And chins first we rammed its wall.
While Rollo bailed out water and Cecil
Worked the motor, I held a lantern high
And howled at the pine wood shore.
Only the fish we had caught could swim,
And they revived in the slosh of our hull.

The storm hooked my cheeks and beat
My voice back. It swallowed up my light.
It rose faster than our buckets and washed
The motor out. Our fish began to swim,
And we began to sink. We despaired,
We cursed fish, water, storm, and world.
We defied nine planets and the cosmos.

Then a great voice said, "Rub-a-dub-dub!"
Behold, our boat rose, water drained,
And the storm uncapped and split above
Our heads! Fish suffered in the hull again
And we sailed off believing, believing.

Zimmer Drunk and Alone,
Dreaming of Old Football Games

I threw the inside of my gizzard out, splashing
Down the steps of that dark football stadium
Where I had gone to celebrate the ancient games.
But I had been gut-blocked and cut down
By a two-ton guard in one quarter of my fifth.
Fireflies broke and smeared upon my eyes,
And the half-moon spiraled on my corneas.
Between spasms the crickets beat halftime to
My tympanum, and stars twirled like fire batons
Inside the darkness. The small roll at my gut's end,
Rising like a cheer, curled up intestines to the stomach,
Quaking to my gullet, and out my tongue again.
Out came old victories, defeats, and scoreless ties,
Out came all the quarters of my fifth,
Until exhausted, my wind gone and teeth sour,
I climbed the high fence out of that dark stadium,
Still smarting from the booing and hard scrimmage.
I zigzagged down the street, stiff-arming buildings,
And giving flashy hip fakes to the lamp posts.
I cut for home, a veteran broken field drunkard,
With my bottle tucked up high away from fumbles.

Zimmer's Love Poem after a Hard Dream

I

In my most spectacular, technicolored dream
The great leaves slap my eyelids
As I smash through vegetation in pursuit
Of my rutting lady. My meat extends
And wavers like a palm log as I see
Her hard cheeks grinding through the bushes,
Her leg muscles bunching,
And breasts sliding like volcanos. Oh sun!
My lady would crush me if she got advantage,
But I stun her with a great stone
And she goes down on her back,
Roaring like a hairy brontosaurus.
Oh then it is I spread her,
And crushed between her incredible thighs,
As pterosaurs clack and duckbills belch,
I raise the human race within my loins
And fire it off to home!

II

All my dreams are for you,
All the glimmers of my organs
Burning into warm humus,
All the doorways like suddenly
Blossoming arbors that you
Appear in, the sun that
You leaf in, the paths down
Which you diminish in anger

And the rain in which you swell,
Wind full of risings and fallings,
Shadows full of the memory
Of them, these are for you.
I am the shrub that shelters
The neat rows of our garden,
You are the inside of my poems,
The light side of my leaves.
Together we graft our love
Quietly onto the world.

from

The Zimmer Poems (1976)

"There was things which he stretched, but mainly he told the truth."

Huckleberry Finn on Mark Twain

In grade school I wondered
Why I had been born
To wrestle in the ashy puddles
With my square nose
Streaming mucus and blood,
My knuckles puffed from combat
And the old nun's ruler.
I feared everything: God,
Learning, and my schoolmates.
I could not count, spell, or read.
My report card proclaimed
These scarlet failures.
My parents wrung their loving hands.
My guardian angel wept constantly.

But I could never hide anything.
If I peed my pants in class
The puddle was always quickly evident,
My worst mistakes were at
The blackboard for Jesus and all
The saints to see.
                    Even now
When I hide behind elaborate mask
It is always known that I am Zimmer,
The one who does the messy papers
And fractures all his crayons,
Who spits upon the radiators
And sits all day in shame
Outside the office of the principal.

What Zimmer Would Be

When asked, I used to say,
"I want to be a doctor,"
Which is the same thing
As a child saying,
"I want to be a priest,"
Or
"I want to be a magician,"
Which is the laying on
Of hands, the vibrations,
The rabbit in the hat,
Or the body in the cup,
The curing of the sick
And the raising of the dead.

"Fix and fix, you're all better,"
I would say
To the neighborhood wounded
As we fought the world war
Through the vacant lots of Ohio.
"Fix and fix, you're all better,"
And they would rise
To fight again.
                    But then
I saw my aunt die slowly of cancer
And a man struck down by a car.

All along I had really
Wanted to be a poet,
Which is, you see, almost
The same thing as saying,
"I want to be a doctor,"

"I want to be a priest,"
Or
"I want to be a magician."
All along, without realizing it,
I had wanted to be a poet.

Fix and fix, you're all better.

One for the Ladies at the Troy Laundry
Who Cooled Themselves for Zimmer

The ladies at the Troy Laundry pressed
And pressed in the warm fog of their labor.
They cooled themselves at the windows,
Steam rising from their gibbous skins
As I dawdled home from school.
In warmer weather they wore no blouses
And if I fought the crumbling coke pile
To the top, they laughed and waved
At me, billowy from their irons.

Oh man, the ladies at the Troy Laundry
Smelled like cod fish out of water
And yet the very fur within their armpits
Made me rise wondering and small.

Father Animus and Zimmer

Father Animus asked who broke
The window in the sacristy,
I went head-on into evil,
Lying through my new incisors.

Holy Ghost moaned in my guts.
The light bulbs swayed on
Their cords in the Parish
As each freckle on my face
Became a venial sin.

Father Animus asked his question,
My answer tangled in memories
Of ardor in the cozy parish:

How springtime I would swing up
Into dogwood trees in the churchyard,
Let the dark eyes of blossoms read
Me like a breviary. Summertime
I ran the baselines as though
They were shadows of the spire.

In fall, exploring the attic
Of the old grade school,
I became my own history in
The dust, finding my father's
Initials carved in a broken desk,
My aunts' and uncles' first communions
Crumbling in antique records.

One winter, when the janitor
Had sprained his ankle, I climbed
Up inside the steeple to free
The bell rope, rung after rung,
Through drafts and timberings.
Bats retreated, wind screeched
Outside through the slate shingles.

I felt I was rising in the head of
Father Animus, through warnings
And pronouncements, his strict,
Reluctant love diminishing as
I aspired, choked, deprived
Of space as I climbed higher.

Father Animus asked who
Broke the sacristy window
And the cross on the spire,
Tucking in its legs,
Flew away in sorrow.

The Sweet Night Bleeds from Zimmer

Imbellis, the bully, catches me in dark
With no sunlight I can squirm through.
His body uncoils its frustrations,
Fists plunge like the last stones
Of a landslide.
                        Pain flies
To my surfaces as though it had
Always been there waiting
For Imbellis to challenge it out.
My skin folds back in slots and tabs
And the sweet night bleeds from my face.

Imbellis catches me in a dark place,
His jaws and pincers grinding.
I feel my brains sucked out of my head,
My heart clutched in his claws,
Remembering and still trying to beat.
I am ground up and spat into the weeds,
The sweet night is bleeding from my skull.

Imbellis catches me in a dark place
And stars descend to coil about my head,
Buzzing about my gravity, sinking
Their stingers in my lips and eyelids.
In the trees each twig and sucker
Is pointing at a separate fire.
How could I have forgotten all these stars?

Stars in the desert faded at dawn;
Then the flash and shock wave rammed
Sand in my face, uprooted cactus,

Blasted animals, birds from the sky.
Afterwards, under the fireball
And faint stars, we wanted to kick
Dead rabbits, throw stones at each other,
Call each other sons-of-bitches.

Once on a dark still lake I dropped
My line between the stars and prayed
For fish in the midst of night.
The small pickerel swallowed my hook
And when I ripped it out the fish
Screamed like a wounded rabbit.
I rowed my boat in out of the dark,
Churning the galaxies and nebulae,
Spoiling the perfect night.

Imbellis caught me in a dark place,
He won't back off and let me be.
I look for a place to hide under
Mother's navel, behind father's penis.
But I can't remember who I am.
Someone wounded and breathing hard,
Trying to become the earth; sorry man
Remembering each cruelty under the stars;
Someone wagging submission forever.

Cecil, Zimmer, and the Man-Made Lake

The dam was built in
A month and the river
Mixed with the creeks
And accrued.
          "Big fish!"
Cecil said, oiling our reels,
Checking our lines. In a week
A shallow lake had formed;
Ten days more it rose above
The tree tops in the valley.

"Just like filling the tub,"
Cecil said, "try flies first, Zimmer,
Then spinners, spoons, and plugs."
We tried them all. No good.
Then baited our hooks with worms,
Shiners, frogs, and salmon eggs,
Until the lake rose up to
The level of our aspirations.

"Tomorrow we troll," said Cecil,
"Then gig, jig, use electric rods!"
But next day the lake had filled
Our basement with excrement,
Old tires, and rusty cans; the kitchen
Filled, then the living room.
It rose to the second floor and
Filled our beds.

"Kill the bastards
With your hands!" said Cecil.
"Grab them by the gills and
Beat their goddamned scales off!"
But we had time only to swim
Up the chimney and paddle
Like hell for shore.

A Zimmershire Lad

Oh what a lad was Zimmer
    Who would rather swill than think,
Who grew to fat from trimmer,
    While taking ale to drink.

Now his stomach hangs so low,
    And now his belt won't hook,
Now his cheeks go to and fro
    When he leaps across a brook.

Oh lads, ere your flesh decay,
    And your sight grows dimmer,
Beware the ale foam in your way
    Or you will end like Zimmer.

Zumer Is Icumen In

Zumer is icumen in,
Lewdly sing whohoo:
Floweth head and gloweth red
And bringth the nuhdie, too.
Sing whohoo!
Owlhe bloteth after ram,
Druleth over calfe cu;
Bumper riseth, butte sizeth;
More he sing whohoo.
Whohoo   Whohoo!
Wel sing whohoo nu!
Sing whohoo nu! Sing whohoo!
Sing whohoo nu!

The Day Zimmer Lost Religion

The first Sunday I missed Mass on purpose
I waited all day for Christ to climb down
Like a wiry flyweight from the cross and
Club me on my irreverent teeth, to wade into
My blasphemous gut and drop me like a
Red hot thurible, the devil roaring in
Reserved seats until he got the hiccups.

It was a long cold way from the old days
When cassocked and surpliced I mumbled Latin
At the old priest and rang his obscure bell.
A long way from the dirty wind that blew
The soot like venial sins across the school yard
Where God reigned as a threatening
One-eyed triangle high in the fleecy sky.

The first Sunday I missed Mass on purpose
I waited all day for Christ to climb down
Like a playground bully, the cuts and mice
Upon his face agleam, and pound me
Till my irreligious tongue hung out.
But of course He never came, knowing that
I was grown up and ready for Him now.

At least I know my peculiar emptiness,
My vague reality, as though
I'd been stunned by a concrete tit at birth,
Dull as a penny bouncing off a cinder block;
My white socks down over high tops,
Big lugs heavy with gravel and mud.

I always get up in the early morning,
Sit on the drugstore bench in mist,
Drink Dr. Peppers for breakfast until
The boys at the Shell station start
Revving their motors like a pride of lions.
I wait all day for things to cool down,
Watch bread trucks and big rigs
Deliver and depart, pass out of sight
Down the interstate.
                                    I get mad about things:
Shattered safety glass in the streets,
Stupid heat lightning swelling out of trees,
Groove, gash, dent, dog, mosquito, fly;
Once in a while something just froths me,
My anger bursting through my skin,
Slapping surface like the side of a bluegill,
Cold, bony mouth snapping and sucking
At hot air, my eyeballs pivoting
Until I can settle down again.

At night I walk the town, look up
Through the tiny squares of window screens,
Inside squares of pictures and doorframes,
Inside glowing squares of television,

Inside the squares of the windows.
Everything is plumb and solid in the night,
Corners of lamplight fastening things down.
Wherever I move the darkness moves
Because I've become my own shadow.
Crickets tinker with the silence.
I walk in the dark alleys, see stars
Well out of the roofs of buildings.
They swarm and multiply like a mass
Of tiny gnats in my gaze. I wonder,
How many could I see if I watched forever?
Star growing into star, year after year,
New revelations spreading beyond sight,
Massing until they all grow together,
Swelling like heat lightning out of trees.
Then maybe I can live like a bluegill
All the time, full of hunger and purpose,
Cool, trim, quick in the water,
One little muscle waiting to strike.

Leaves of Zimmer

You, Zimmer! Whimpering, heavy, mumbling, lewd;
Does America sing you a sad song?
It is a trifle! Resign yourself!
Nothing is without flaw.
Confess that you feel small buds unclutching again!
Confess that rich sod turns up to you always as your
    lover!
By God! Accept nothing less than this for affection:
The stars dangling like green apples on distant peaks;
Sea foam combing itself through rocks;
No foofoo can strip you of this!
No mountebanks can take this away!
If one is deprived, then all are deprived;
America will love us all or it will not love.
Camerado! Give me your hand.
All of us will go! Boatmen and trappers,
Bridegroom and bride, sailors, and drifters,
Woodsmen, mechanics, preachers, lawyers, fishermen.
We must also raise the insulted and injured.
Even the President will come!
If one of us falls the others must wait;
For lacking one we lack all.
Camerado! My left hand hooks you round the waist.
My right hand points to America.
Let us feel the country under our boot soles;
Let us seek it in the air we breathe.

An Enzyme Poem for Suzanne

What a drag it must be for you!
I slog along, ignoring you like my heart beat.
I gurgle and mold like an old fruit cellar,
Then suddenly you'll walk through a door
And foam me up like ancient cider in heat.
Then I'll fall all about you, blathering
With lost time, making you numb with words,
Wanting to mix our molecules, trying
To tell you of weeks in fifteen minutes.
Sometimes you must wonder what the hell
It is with Zimmer.
                    This is to tell you
That you are my enzymes, my yeast,
All the things that make my cork go pop.

Zimmer Envying Elephants

I have a wide, friendly face
Like theirs, yet I can't hang
My nose like a fractured arm
Nor flap my dishpan ears.
I can't curl my canine teeth,
Swing my tail like a filthy tassel,
Nor make thunder without lightning.

But I'd like to thud amply around
For a hundred years or more,
Stuffing an occasional tree top
Into my mouth, screwing hugely for
Hours at a time, gaining weight,
And slowly growing a few hairs.

Once in a while I'd charge a power pole
Or smash a wall down just to keep
Everybody loose and at a distance.

Zimmer Loathing the Gentry

Their faces are like fine watches
Insinuating jewels.
Their movements can buy or sell you.
When the legs of gentry dance for charity,
Meat splashes in the soups of the poor.
The eyes of gentry are polished and blown,
When they look at you, you are worthless.
The gentry protect their names like hymens,
They suck their names like thumbs,
But they sign their names and something happens.
While, Zimmer, I can write, Zimmer,
All day, and nothing happens.

Death Demonstrates His Presence to Zimmer

I almost strangled on an almond,
Two weeks later I almost drowned.
Twice in a month death said,
"Hello, Zimmer," and showed me
Who is boss. I wanted to yank
His reserved seat out and send
Him clattering, but I was busy
Just trying to stay alive.

I swallowed the almond whole and crossways
And the river tried to swallow me.
By the time we had dislodged each other
My vision doubled and darkened,
And I was on my knees to
Old mortality's parched phalanges.

When I was young I used to spit
In the insufferable eye of death,
Blow him apart with a loaded cigar
And offer him only the wormy apples.

But I had never almost died before.

Twice in a month death touched
My intolerant lungs, and now I feel him
On each frigid wind off the river
That blows blossoms from the almond trees,
In every alien tingle of my fingertips and toes.

Zimmer's Bed

Old bed, you are a garden.
Each night I roll over
And sink through you
Like a root into
Darkness. Now I will
Say goodnight, goodnight.
I have slept on you
So long I forget
How much I love you.
Yet my children and poems
Are sewn in you.
Can you tell me
If they will bloom
And be immortal?
Never mind. Goodnight,
Goodnight.

from

With Wanda: Town and Country Poems (1980)

"She had come into the world like a thing unknown. She had come upon him unawares. She was a danger — a frightful danger. The instinctive mood of fierce determination that had never failed him before the perils of this life added its steady force to the violence of his passion."

Joseph Conrad, *Nostromo*

Wanda Being Beautiful

To be beautiful is to somehow keep
A dozen fires burning at night,
To know that all eyes shining
Out of the trees are afraid of you.
It is to know that every crackle of
A twig, every footfall is a threat,
That desire is greatest from a distance.

To be beautiful is to stay on the move
Through every season, to watch sharply
As you take what you want, but mostly
It is knowing how to choose dry wood,
How to bank your fires against cold.

Wanda and the Fish

She told him that she could not do this thing;
He heard only the rumbling of heavy currents.
She said she wanted to with all her heart
But could not; that everything she had been told
By God and man made this an evil thing to do;
That she loved him, but could not do this thing.

Harking only to cold blood grinding through his meat,
To what the moon whispered as it pressed upon
His back, he went on against her protests.
When it was over he disappeared into the depths.

Still, after all these years, she dreams of him.
He becomes a fish fanning and holding in currents.
She shows herself and he strikes with all his might,
Sand and bits of weed swirl up around them;
He devours her, makes her one with his flesh,
Carries her forever in the folds of his silver brain.

Wanda Dreams of Eli and the Farm

Eli has mud on his shoes;
I watch him pull off the head
Of a chicken as though he is
Plucking a flower and the bird
Dances and flops in its juices,
Smelling like a sweaty pillow.

I am chased by sows in heat
Beneath heavy skies that lower
To strangle the fields; I fall
Into nettles and my blood is sucked
By chiggers.
           The weathervane moans
In the wind, the gray barn squawks
On its nails.
           I lie down in the loft
To await the end of the storm;
In dim light I open like a seed,
Struggle up like a shoot through
Clods and manure into the light
Of fields.
           I feel the thousand
Eyes of the locust as it looms
Above me, its pincers grinding.
Slowly it gnaws my head off and one by one
The colors disappear from the farm.

When I awake the farm is shining
Through cracks in the clapboard.
I open the barndoor and the smell is innocent
And clean like a change of seasons.

Hens cluck, the weathervane struts,
Pigs are cool in their mud;
The barn stands plump and solid
In the day and Eli waves to me,
Smiling from his tidy rows.

Rollo's Miracle

Rollo says, "I can bring down rain."
We say, "Bull crap!" and slug him
On his bicep. But he says,
"Underwear ain't fit to wear!"
And lightning cracks its knuckles,
Thunder pulls the plug out.
Fish could swim in what comes down.

When it lets up we say to Rollo,
"Bull crap, buddy, you got lucky!"
But Wanda is giving Rollo the eye.

"Underwear ain't fit to wear!"
He chants again and clouds uncork,
The river starts to rise.
Wanda takes Rollo by the arm,
They go off to meet the rainbow.

We stand there with the cold rain
Sighing in our socks. Cecil says,
"Underwear ain't fit to wear."
"Underwear ain't fit to wear!"
Shouts Zimmer. Lester whispers,
"Underwear ain't fit to wear."
But that sun shines on and on—
Bright as a fresh dropped egg.

Robyn Hode and Maid Wanda

In somer, when the shawes be sheyne,
    And wodes do sprytly ryng,
Hit is so mery in the leves
    To here the briddis syng.

A yeman lyved amydst these trees,
    By name of Robyn Hode,
A prode and mery outlaw he,
    Yet ful of certaine gude.

One day he boed and arow
    Depe into a grene wode tree,
But Robyn nere fell don when
    The swete barke cryde, "Ah me!"

For in the holowe of the tree
    A wenche hae hidde herself,
The yeman to ploke his arow back
    Wode hae gie al his pelf.

Robyn toke her up from thair
    And bond her wunde sae sorre,
He loked upon her wyth gladde eye
    For she was fare and morre.

Now in the grene wode do they lyve
    With lytel Johnn, Scarloke, and Monke,
Mony a wondrous tyme hae they hadde,
    Ful many more shaftes hae been sonke.

Lester Tells of Wanda and the Big Snow

Some years back I worked a strip mine
Out near Tylersburg. One day it starts
To snow and by two we got three feet.
I says to the foreman, "I'm going home."
He says, "Ain't you stayin' till five?"
I says, "I got to see to my cows,"
Not telling how Wanda was there at the house.
By the time I make it home at four
Another foot is down and it don't quit
Until it lays another. Wanda and me
For three whole days seen no one else.
We tunneled the drifts and slid
Right over the barbed wire, laughing
At how our heartbeats melted the snow.
After a time the food was gone and I thought
I'd butcher a cow, but then it cleared
And the moon come up as sweet as an apple.
Next morning the ploughs got through. It made us sad.
It don't snow like that no more. Too bad.

Lester Tells of the End of Summer

Wanda was having an ugly night,
All drawed and pale in her glow,
Rolling her tired bones in the stars
Through branches of the trees.
We'd drunk wine all day together
And Wanda was worse for the wear.
Pock marks yawed in her cheeks,
Her temples pulled in for dryness.
I was the elm that propped her up
But rotted with the blight myself.
Deep in my trunk I felt the sadness.
My leaves knowed things they couldn't tell,
Yearning to fall and loosen in
Slime and dirt, far below moonshine,
Down in dark where the old people lay.

Dear Wanda (Letter from Rollo)

Dear Wanda,

A month ago the sun disappeared,
Clouds swelled up like giant fungi.
I figured something big was up
So I tore the old barn down
And built myself a ponderous raft,
Hoisting the house to put on top.
I laid in a hundred cases of Stroh's,
Then I gathered animals two-by-two:
The sweet swine and foul goats,
Cattle to breathe me some peace.
I went a long way for alligators—
Mountain lions ate the sheep before
I could get them in. Two turtles,
Two hares in heat, two treefrogs,
And a pair of rutting reindeer.
The snow geese boarded each other
In anticipation of their nest!
Wanda, I had big plans for us as well.
But as the rain began to fall
I could not find you anywhere.
Water's up to my armpits now,
Buffalo and plough horses kick
Boards right out of my keel.
Termites gnaw at the strakes.
But why should I give a damn?
Wanda, where the hell were you?

Still fondly,
Rollo

Dear Wanda (Letter from Zimmer)

Dear Wanda,

Last night I dreamt you were Emily Dickinson.
I waited for you, uneasy in your parlor.
After many hours you came into the room.
You were ill, your temples sunken,
A light sweat stippled your upper lip.
Still, you made me nervous. You handed
This poem to me and left again:

> This was my letter to a Moor—
> Writ in mad divinest sense—
> From a life closed twice before
> That made my lines so lean and tense
>
> The words I chose were hard and few—
> Of liquor, heather, snake, and claw—
> Of other things I never knew
> And did not see—but saw

Wanda, I have remembered
Every line. The cadence has
Frightened me, rhymes leer
At my uneasiness. Please do not
Come into my dreams again.

Love,
Zimmer

Gus in the Streets

On hot nights the whole city
Shares industry, air tastes of
Tarnished coins, cinders sparkle
Through the lamplight and settle
In the cups of my molars.
Even television grits behind
My eyes, so I walk out into
The smutty streets past alleys
Of old bones and glass, past
The marquees of skin shows
Into the neighborhood of rooms.
Here, where air bites hardest
Into my flesh, I imagine that
Wanda calls me from a doorway,
Her eyes smoldering with consent.

Later, upstairs with an old whore
And tasting ashes again, I wonder
Why Wanda never kept promises.
Why her face, so full of cozy signals,
Had never really intended all
The things I thought it meant.

Thurman's Slumping Blues

One day out in right field
The ball went by me quicker
Than a flushed-out quail.
I wagged my glove at it
But what I got was wind.
Then I fell down like a fool.
Fans stung me harder than
A swarm of bald-faced hornets.
That was what started
The whole damned thing.

I felt the sap run out of my knees,
Looked at my hands, they smelled of fish.
Wanda was up there in the box seats,
Sitting on a whole school of mackerel.

We dropped in the standings.
Pitchers pulled the string
And tied me up in knots.
I went left when I should have gone right.
Wanda commenced to acting skittish.
Today I woke up and she was gone.
Over my steak and eggs
The paper tells me that
This is last place.

Zimmer's Last Gig

Listening to hard bop,
I stayed up all night
Just like good times.
I broke the old waxes
After I'd played them:
Out of Nowhere, Mohawk,
Star Eyes, Salt Peanuts,
Confirmation, one-by-one;
Bird, Monk, Bud, Klook, Diz,
All dead, all dead anyway,
As clay around my feet.

Years ago I wanted to
Take Wanda to Birdland,
Certain that the music
Would make her desire me,
That after a few sets
She would give in to
Rhythm and sophistication.
Then we could slip off
Into the wee hours with
Gin, chase, and maryjane,
Check into a downtown pad,
Do some fancy jitterbugging
Between the lilywhites.

But Wanda was no quail.
Bud could have passed
Out over the keys,
Bird could have shot
Up right on the stand,

Wanda would have missed
The legends. The band
Could have riffed
All night right by
Her ear, she never
Would have bounced.

Dear Wanda (Letter from Christiaan)

Dear Wanda,

I go out in the long nights to
Stars again, measure and track
The dazzle, sense numbers meshing
Like gears in the ancient voids.
I feel my excited body try to shine
Out to those farflung corners.

I always look for you in the lens,
See galaxies coiling and spreading,
The flexing of the nebulae,
Startled vacuums of black holes.
Scanning the horizon, I pretend
That you are the great star blinking
On the north rim, though I know
It is only Arcturus descending.

I swear mine is the only warmth in
The universe, the one intelligent sign.
The rest is only frigid silence.

But, Wanda, when I seek you in
The stars, I remember all our warm,
Deliberate movements on the tracks
Of the great night. I still wonder
Where you might be in all this glister.

Love,
Christiaan

Gus Sees Wanda Drinking

When she was drunk
The veins pumped up
In her forehead.
Full lips slathered
The foam of wine.
Once, in her anger,
She spit into my face,
But I did not flinch
Nor wipe it away.
Her fingers grew bony
And red, scrabbling
Like crabs on the bottle.

Once I found her weeping
In the street at dawn.
When I tried to help her
She broke her glass
And threatened to lay
My damp cheeks open.

Nothing had gone right.
She was easy and cheap,
Her perfume was violent,
Her make-up eroded
With sweat and tears.
She was certain
She would die unloved.

To be a woman was hell.
Would I *please* give her
Some change and go away?

She would come home soon.
The sun was coming up.
She needed to rest.
If I gave her money
She would not drink anymore.
She would buy coffee,
Wash her face and never
Frighten me again.

Dear Wanda (Letter from Cecil)

Dear Wanda,

Worrying about you all the time,
I could just as well be drowning.
I went to see your act last night,
Sat down on my piles, in the doldrums,
My soft teeth aching in the grind,
Eyeballs burning through bifocals.
Then you floated into the spotlight,
Hands unfolding, folding like sting rays.
The cymbal started to sizzle as
You slipped out of clothes and floated
Them to the sharks in the audience.
The circles of your thighs, calves,
Bob and weave of belly, breasts,
Making the whole room sigh and sweat.

And you would give these things away
So easily! The secrets all of us
Had burned to see, you revealed as
Lightly as a perch can lay its eggs.
Even the band saw everything!

Wanda, I went out into the night,
My eyeballs rolled in currents,
Cold surf fired my teeth up,
My chill heart drained with the knowledge
That you aren't precious anymore.

So long,
Cecil

Zimmer and the Ghost

We are like the masters of a lost dog,
Suddenly remembering all the sweet things
That she was. Wanda is dead and
None of us really knew who she was.

She was the best of us,
Always had courage to depart,
To frighten us by moving beyond bounds,
But now she has gone too far.
She will not come to us again.

Yesterday I thought I saw a ghost in
The strangled light of the ancient field.
"Z i m m e r !" it lisped at me
As it fumed out of loose sod,
Its leering face a bag
Of working maggots and its hands
And nails clacking and constricting.
"Z i m m e r !" it called.

I thought it was an elm stump beckoning,
A fence post or a buckthorn blowing,
Even as I hoped that it was Wanda.
But as I walked toward it, my left eye
Twitched, my fingertips froze,
And my heart rammed the inside
Of my ribs.

It was nothing, of course:
And I had wanted it to be Wanda,
Had wanted to be baffled again!

Wanda, when I am a ghostly spirit
Rising wormy and long-buried to walk
The earth, I'll never toy with victims
Nor simply be a flicker in
The corner of their frightened eyes.
I will rise up in all my pearly,
Frozen essence, grinding my snags
And moaning like an albino walrus.
I will look my victim squarely under
Her sweating eyebrows, and ask,
"D o   y o u   l o v e   m e ?"
And if she answers yes, then—
And only then—will I fade.

from

Family Reunion (1983)

Once as a Child I Had Bad Dreams

Lightning ignited the treetops,
Funnels dropped like fast freights,
One writhed and struck at me.
I looked up its eye to the fires
Of hell and woke screaming.
There was my mother holding me.
A steam tent hissed in my room.
A faint light. I was very warm.
She sang a French song for me,
Stroked my brow with love,
Gave me the comfort of woman.

Now I will make this poem with a wish
That it might assume her fear,
That it would sing the storms away
From her, that it could die for her,
Who has become her own suffering.
I wish this poem could be her pain
So she could walk away from it,
Returning to dignity and sureness.
I would have it fill the lonely void
She told me women always feel
Beyond the comprehension of all men.

Irene Gogle

Bugs lived in her hair.
Her one dress was weary.
The nuns were kind
But kept their distance.
When she read aloud
The tedious clock ticked
Between her words.

"Go-go!" we called her.
"Go-go is your girlfriend!"
—when we wished to insult
Another boy. I loathed her
Aloud with the rest;
Once, on a dare, pushed
Her into a classmate so
He could feel her breasts.
The nun broke a yardstick
Over our cowering backs.

On the playground she would
Stand alone by the fence,
Bouncing a dirty tennis ball,
Pretending to be cheerful.

Why should she come to
My mind again? I say words
To my grade-school son:
Kindness, love, compassion.
I pray to God for definitions.

for Erik

/ 72

The Eisenhower Years

Flunked out and laid-off,
Zimmer works for his father
At Zimmer's Shoes for Women.
The feet of old women awaken
From dreams, they groan and rub
Their hacked-up corns together.
At last they stand and walk in agony
Downtown to Zimmer's fitting stool
Where he talks to the feet,
Reassures and fits them with
Blissful ties in medium heels.

Home from work he checks the mail
For greetings from his draft board.
After supper he listens to Brubeck,
Lays out with a tumbler of Thunderbird,
Cigarettes and *From Here to Eternity*.

That evening he goes out to the bars,
Drinks three pitchers of Stroh's,
Ends up in the wee hours leaning
On a lamp post, his tie loosened,
Fedora pushed back on his head,
A Chesterfield stuck to his lips.

All of complacent America
Spreads around him in the night,
Nothing is moving in this void,
Only the feet of old women,
Twitching and shuffling in pain.

Zimmer sighs and takes a drag.
Exhales through his nostrils.
He knows nothing and feels little.
He has never been anywhere
And fears where he is going.

The Ancient Wars

Dear Imbellis:

When I think of the old days
I start to bleed again,
Recalling my terrified exits;
The alleys and swamps I hid in;
Your fists exploding in my face
And light fog of concussions.
I wonder, old bull, old turk,
Old hammer, if we passed
Each other on the street,
Would your anger spill out
Again over your eye rims?
Would your ears redden
Like a rooster's wattle,
Would you knock my bridge
Back down my throat and beat
My glasses back into my dim eyes?
I like to think that
By now you have relented,
That some woman or work
Has doused your fires,
That if we met again we would
Slap each other on the back
And laugh about the ancient wars.
Imbellis, old bravo, super pug,
Could we be friends now?
Would you let me forgive you?

Peace,
Zimmer

Dear Zimmer,

Remember how you loved the Friday Night Fights?
That was always you and me in the ring,
Circling, jabbing, throwing classy combinations
Until the abrupt explosion, my fists crashing
Down like boulders, your body suddenly limp;
You collapsing as a hammered cow into
Your own spit and blood as the crowd
Came to its feet growling and hooting;
You on the canvas flapping and quaking,
You crawling up the ropes to your feet
And me sledging you down again
And you screaming at the television,
"Stop it! Stop it!" Remember?

Zimmer start sweating again.
I am waiting for you still,
Maybe around the next corner.
One day you'll come
Blundering into my sights again;
When you do I'll clean your clock
But good, shred your cheeks,
Roll your bloody teeth,
Crunch your jewels and punch
Your dim lights out forever.

Yours,
Imbellis

The Duke Ellington Dream

Of course Zimmer was late for the gig.
Duke was pissed and growling at the piano,
But Jeep, Brute, Rex, Cat, and Cootie
All moved down on the chairs
As Zimmer walked in with his tenor.
Everyone knew that the boss had arrived.

Duke slammed out the downbeat for Caravan
And Zimmer stood up to take his solo.
The whole joint suddenly started jiving,
Chicks came up to the bandstand
To hang their lovelies over the rail.
Duke was sweating but wouldn't smile
Through chorus after chorus after chorus.

It was the same with Satin Doll,
Do Nothing Till You Hear from Me,
Warm Valley, In a Sentimental Mood;
Zimmer blew them so they would stay played.

After the final set he packed
His horn and was heading out
When Duke came up and collared him.
"Zimmer," he said. "You most astonishing ofay!
You have shat upon my charts,
But I love you madly."

The Great House

Over and over it happens, my wife and I are
Out walking, we come to a great stone house
Built into a hillside. We are young again;
All things seem possible on this perfect day.
Suddenly we know that the house is ours!
We enter in joy, exulting in what we own:
Circular staircases, niches, ballrooms,
A dozen rooms full of leatherbound books,
Lace curtains, puppet theatres, daguerreotypes,
Chests full of doilies and ancient manuscripts,
Hand printing presses, bowls of potpourri;
There are antique cribs, rocking chairs,
A canopied bed. We could start our lives again!
All windows swing open to singing birds and trees
Through which we see a whitewashed, sunlit city.

At night, after a lingering dinner and wine,
Lieder and string quartets by candle glow,
We ascend the tower, open the skylight
And turn the huge reflector into position.
The shimmer that we see has traveled for eons.
Under the circling stars, the birds against
The moon, with the vast rooms breathing
Beneath us, we know that the only sadness
In the world will be to leave this house.

A Final Affection

I love the accomplishments of trees,
How they try to restrain great storms
And pacify the very worms that eat them.
Even their deaths seem to be considered.

I fear for trees, loving them so much.
I am nervous about each scar on bark,
Each leaf that browns. I want to
Lie in their crotches and sigh,
Whisper of sun and rains to come.

Sometimes on summer evenings I step
Out of my house to look at trees
Propping darkness up to the silence.

When I die I want to slant up
Through those trunks so slowly
I will see each rib of bark, each whorl;
Up through the canopy, the subtle veins
And lobes touching me with final affection;
Then to hover above and look down
One last time on the rich upliftings,
The circle that loves the sun and moon,
To see at last what held the darkness up.

When Angels Came to Zimmer

One morning a great gaggle slid
Down through holes in clouds,
Twirling like maple seeds
Through trees to the windowscreen.
Fervent as new tussock moths,
They flapped and dashed themselves,
Smearing their heavenly dust,
Until Zimmer, in pity and alarm,
Opened to let them into his study.
They flew in with smiles and sighs,
Making him bashful, as if a dozen
Gorgeous chorus girls had suddenly
Pranced into the room.
                    They perched on
Bookshelves, cigar stubs, and beer cans;
One even tried to sit on Zimmer's lap.
All day they danced the lindy,
And some, not knowing better, dabbled
Their darling toes in the toilet bowl.
They sang chorus after chorus of
"Stardust" and "Moonlight in Vermont,"
Constantly touching and stroking Zimmer.
Then at day's end, as if someone
Had rung a bell, they stood to sing
A final chorus of "Deep Purple."
With a whoosh of air and expensive perfume,
They fluttered from the room and ascended.
Zimmer stepped out to watch them rise
And flapped his dirty hankie at the stars.

Work

To have done it thirty years
Without question! Yet I tell myself
I am grateful for all work;
At noon in my air-conditioned office
With a sandwich and a poem,
I try to recollect nature;
But a clerk comes in with papers
To be signed. I tell myself
The disruption does not matter;
It is all work: computer runs,
Contracts, invoices, poems; the same
As breaking shells, hunting woods,
Making pots or gathering grain.
Jazzmen even refer to sex as work.
Some primitive people believe
That death is work. When my wife asks
What I am doing, I always answer,
I am working, working, working.

Now I know I will spend the rest
Of my life trying for perfect work,
A work as rare as aurora borealis,
So fine it will make all other work
Seem true, that will last as long
As words will last. At home
In my room, I mumble to myself
Over my poems; over supper I talk
To myself; as I carpenter or paint

Or carry the groceries up the steps,
I am speaking words to myself.
"What are you doing?" my children ask.
I am working, working, working.

Zimmer Imagines Heaven

I sit with Joseph Conrad in Monet's garden.
We are listening to Yeats chant his poems,
A breeze stirs through Thomas Hardy's moustache,
John Skelton has gone to the house for beer,
Wanda Landowska lightly fingers a harpsichord,
Along the spruce tree walk Roberto Clemente and
Thurman Munson whistle a baseball back and forth.
Mozart chats with Ellington in the roses.

Monet smokes and dabs his canvas in the sun,
Brueghel and Turner set easels behind the wisteria.
The band is warming up in the Big Studio:
Bean, Brute, Bird, and Serge on saxes,
Kai, Bill Harris, Lawrence Brown trombones,
Little Jazz, Clifford, Fats, Diz on trumpets,
Klook plays drums, Mingus bass, Bud the piano.
Later Madam Schuman-Heink will sing Schubert,
The monks of Benedictine Abbey will chant.
There will be more poems from Emily Dickinson,
James Wright, John Clare, Walt Whitman.
Shakespeare rehearses players for *King Lear.*

At dusk Alice Toklas brings out platters
Of sweetbreads, Salad Livonière,
And a tureen of Gazpacho of Málaga.
After the meal Brahms passes fine cigars.
God comes then, radiant with a bottle of cognac,
She pours generously into the snifters,
I tell Her I have begun to learn what

Heaven is about. She wants to hear.
It is, I say, being thankful for eternity.
Her smile is the best part of the day.

for Merrill Leffler

from

The Great Bird of Love
(1989)

"Keep your eyes on the fellow at the piano. The sparrow.
He don't know nothing, but just keep your eyes on him
and we'll all be together on what's going down."

Count Basie

The Dream of My Second Conscription

The images form with unendurable sadness,
You and the children, helpless in despair,
As I wave goodbye from a troop bus.
How could a dream show more of loss?
My children, who grow away from me
In their lives, weep in this dream
For need of me. It is almost more
Than I can bear, that I would
Go again and not be with you,
That I would stand in freezing rain
And be assured of my inhumanity,
That I would go again to be
Taught the insult of how to kill.
Yet how could a dream so terrible
Show more of love? This is an illusion
So fraught with calamity that,
Were I to waken and not find you
Here beside me, surely I would die.

The Origins of Love

The first time I saw her, light was falling,
Air was rich like the last days of autumn.
Despite her dazzle and warmth, I was melancholy,
As I have always been in the presence of beauty.

From then on I tried every day to be decent.
When I was crass, her lovely shoulders
Drooped like finished tulips in the garden.
I did not want to wait, and yet I waited
As I had never done before, and surely
In time the delicate snows began to fall.

So the glory of my restraint inspired me.
I became eloquent, attentive, civilized.
Times I had to say goodbye to her became
The greatest burdens of my onerous life.

Although she gave me no reason to doubt,
I was constantly afraid, I thought perhaps
A god might come and take her from me.
Somehow it pleased me that others admired her,
Yet it made my knuckles
Turn white like worried children.

Two Drinking Songs

ZIMMER REPUDIATES BEER

It is an idiot's way to die,
Therefore when you next see me
I will look like a cactus needle
Sans body, liquid, and weight,
But keen enough to make you pay.
No more will I raise the glass
And swallow till I see the froth.
I swear by the Muse that I will
Cease this slaughtering of brain cells
And no longer build this stomach
Brick by brick and glass by glass
Until the lights grow dim.
Though in summer it cools me
And in winter it warms my soul,
I herewith deny this perfection.

ZIMMER RESISTING TEMPERANCE

Some people view life as food served
By a psychopath. They do not trust it.
But Zimmer expects always to be happy.
Puzzled by melancholy, he pours a reward
And loves this world relentlessly.

Years ago he saw a snake suck light from
A frog's eyes. Now with his drink in hand,
He swallows and feels his own brain implode,
The vessels in his nose begin to glow.

Each day he plans to end up squatting like
Mahatma Gandhi with a glass of unsweetened tea.
He wishes he looked like a Rouault Christ.
But who says Zimmer should not compensate himself?
Though worn out at both ends,
He regards his happy middle,
His gilded eyes in the mirror.

Someday he may fall face down
In the puke of his own buoyancy,
But while the world and his body
Are breaking down,
Zimmer will hold his glass up.

The Poets' Strike

On the stroke of this midnight
Let us cover our typewriters,
Throw down all pens and papers,
Build kindling fires in oil drums.
Let there be no more poems,
Not one more metaphor nor image,
No loose nor strict iambics,
No passion, anger, laughter.
Let no one cheat nor scab,
No furtive peeks in notebooks,
No secret scribbling in closets,
Let us dwell together in a void
Removed from beauty and truth.

Then let us see what happens,
How many trees will blight,
How earth wobbles and fractures,
Words loosen and fall from dictionaries.
People will move through life
Like worms swallowing
And excreting their tedious passage.
They'll beg us for one crippled line,
One near rhyme, one feeble dream,
And they will be so sorry
They will pay and pay and pay.

for Rod Jellema

The moon rolls down a low branch
And dips itself into the bear's vision;
Bear grows honey-eyed and torpid,
Scarcely makes its way back to
The hollow before it falls
Into deepest slumber. No matter
How much the stars fuss,
They cannot pry open its eyes.
Even the sun takes a turn,
But bear belongs to the moon.
It dreams of sweet light,
A syrup as radiant as fox fire,
It does not dream of us.
When the bear thinks,
It does not think of us.
Even if we slaughter it,
Eat its meat, wear its coat,
We cannot become the bear.
Though bear is greater
Than we are, it does
Not wish to harm us.
Now the bear is waking up,
The moon releases its hold.
Bear mumbles and farts,
Scratches its navel.
Even after long dreaming
It knows more than we know.
If we think of water, earth,
Fire, or wind, the bear
Is wiser than we are.
This is a difficult lesson,

But we cannot dwell on it,
Dare not let it perturb us.
If we think of numbers,
God, words, the universe,
Bear knows more than we know.

The Sounds of Magpie

Nobody ever owned magpie,
But now he is down in the berm.
His friends hold raucous wake
Above him before they drift away.
Magpie needs no undertaker,
Has always been dressed for the end.

Magpie attempted to live a good life,
Built well and saved bright things he loved.
He tried speaking gently to his children,
But forever ended saying, raw-raw-raw!

He loved his mate and chased with her,
Kissed her with a clack when they met;
As they made love he'd go, aw-aw-aw!

Magpie would get sick with the drink;
He picked dead flesh off an old cow's back,
Flew to a tree and threw up, aargh!

When magpie was young he said, now-now-now!
When he grew old he gargled with glass,
Ground his beak and said, fuck you, fuck you!

Magpie grew quiet, knew something was up,
He let the young birds chatter and chase.
One day he went to feed on the road;
When he got smacked he said, oof!

The Old Trains at Night

In the forties and fifties
It seemed like every time trains
Hauled out of town at night,
They rolled into my flawless sleep.
Awake, I loved to watch them come in
Like big dogs breathing hard,
Grinding their cheeks at the stations.

Then the first diesels came through,
Piddling on crossties and smelling of crap.
The damned things bred like dingy rabbits
Till by 1960 all the real trains were scrap.
Now the world belongs to bloodless bastards
Who tell us all the steam trains are gone.

But on rainy nights I hear them
Mope around, mumble to themselves,
Slipping on glazed rails and belching.
I wake to hear them hooting at
Each other over the forlorn distances
And I start pulling for them, too.

They were finest in winter when
They showed what they could do,
Slamming their way through huge drifts,
Chests heaving, great hearts pounding.

But they ran best on moonlight,
Heaving out steam to secret wildflowers,
They slid through ground fog and hauled
Themselves panting into our dreams.

for Gary Gildner

How Zimmer Will Be Reborn

Make it an ancient rookery,
A crumbling abbey in York,
A place where God's old slaves,
Cistercians, still dwell in
The spirit of dingy birds.

Make it a grizzled sky
Rolling over broken walls.
Make the air chill and wet,
Desire for warmth overwhelming.

Despite the outrage
Of righteous flocks
I will begin to claw my
Way up the worn stones
Toward a reechy nest
Tucked into a cranny.

When the mother rook
Goes to forage I will
Slip into the pocket
Of moldy leaves and sticks,
Snuggle down amongst
Warm, ticking eggs.

When she returns I will
Listen to her tender croaks,
Feel myself being coaxed out
By the song of woman,
The desire to come forth

Overwhelming, to rise,
Strutting and screeching
At anything that moves,
Guarding my few square yards.

Yellow Sonnet

Zimmer no longer wishes to write
About the dimming of his lights,
Recounting all his small terrors.
Instead he tells of brilliance,
Walking home from first grade
In springtime, light descending
To hold itself and dazzle him
In an outburst of dandelions.
It was then he learned that
He would always love yellow,
Its warm dust on his knuckles,
The memory of gathering pieces
To carry home in his lunch pail
As a love gift for his mother.

Sitting with Lester Young

Dusk must become your light
If you want to see Lester Young.
So Zimmer sits beside him at
His window in the Alvin Hotel.
Pres is blue beyond redemption.
His tenor idle on the table,
He looks down at the street,
Drinking his gin and port.
Buildings slice the last light
From the day. If Pres could
Shuffle into a club again like
A wounded animal, he would
Blow his ultimate melancholy,
But nights belong to others now.
Zimmer can only watch Pres
In the half-light of his sadness,
Old whispers slipping around,
Words into melodies,
As holy silence means the most.

for Michael S. Harper

The Tenth Circle

*"More than three (3) health emergency calls in one month from
apartment to switchboard shall be conclusive evidence to
landlord that occupant is not capable of independent living.
Landlord can then have tenant moved to such health care
facility as available."*

Dear Dad,

Do not fall for the third time,
Or if you do, tell no one.
Hunch over your agony and
Make it your ultimate secret.
You have done this before.
Shrug, tell a joke, go on.
If an ambulance slips up
Quietly to the back door
Do not get on. They mean to
Take you to the tenth circle
Where everyone is turned in
One direction, piled like cordwood
Inside the cranium of Satan
So that only the light of
Television shines in their eyes.
Dad, call if you need help,
But do not let them take you
Easily to this place where
They keep the motor idling
On the long black car, where if
Someone cries out in the night
Only the janitor comes.

Love,
Paul

The Explanation

Before his last fires were dowsed,
Before the irreversible stillness,
My father stormed against equivocation,
Heaving against tubes and wires
Until they had to bind him down.

The doctors asked for explanation.
He called for pencil and paper,
Angrily scribbled for a moment,
Then wrote in his clearest,
Most commanding hand, "I am dead."

Winter

My mother sits alone
In the gloaming.
Out her window
Streetlamps chill
In the distance,
Snow begins to flitter
Through their light.
I come to hold
Her hand, to sit
With the shadows
In her room.
I am born and dead
In an instant.

The Place

Once in your life you pass
Through a place so pure
It becomes tainted even
By your regard, a space
Of trees and air where
Dusk comes as perfect ripeness.
Here the only sounds are
Sighs of rain and snow,
Small rustlings of plants
As they unwrap in twilight.
This is where you will go
At last when coldness comes.
It is something you realize
When you first see it,
But instantly forget.
At the end of your life
You remember and dwell in
Its faultless light forever.

The Great Bird of Love

I want to become a great night bird
Called The Zimmer, grow intricate gears
And tendons, brace my wings on updrafts,
Roll them down with a motion
That lifts me slowly into the stars
To fly above the troubles of the land.
When I soar the moon will shine past
My shoulder and slide through
Streams like a luminous fish.
I want my cry to be huge and melancholy,
The undefiled movement of my wings
To fold and unfold on rising gloom.

People will see my silhouette from
Their windows and be comforted,
Knowing that, though oppressed,
They are cherished and watched over,
Can turn to kiss their children,
Tuck them into their beds and say:
     Sleep tight.
     No harm tonight,
     In starry skies
     The Zimmer flies.

from

Big Blue Train (1993)

"A smart brakie keeps a firm grip on a grab iron
or stanchion when he's riding the caboose platform.
Inside, some roads have thoughtfully provided handrails
running the full length of the hack. But the general rule
is 'sit down, brother,' when the rumble of free slack
comes surging down a mile of manifest."

Railroad Magazine, August 1949

The Persistence of Fatherhood

Yesterday the autumn finished.
I began raking it into piles
Around the house. Sue came out
And called from the distance.
I cupped my ears but could not hear
Through bare winds and branches rattling.

I thought she said,
"Your father's on the phone,"
And started walking toward
The house, until I remembered
He's been dead for five years.

Then last night this dream:
Suddenly leaves were children's clothing,
Blue jeans, caps, and flannel shirts.
I raked them up, bent over by sadness,
Fatherhood all used up and gone,
Playthings and storytimes gone,
I swept and piled, doing my duties,
Only this caretaking left to do.

Fog in the Valley

Old combines dither and cough,
Cows amble vaguely into pastures,
Fences vibrate out to the end
Of their stringency, but all
This occurs beneath an opaque sea.

Last week in Manhattan a man
Walked up to me on a foggy morning
And asked for money. When I told
Him I had no change he exploded,
"Man, how do you think I *feel*,
Having to ask you for a handout?"

The fog unloosens and slips
In patches up hillsides.
Hawks are first to ease off
Their perches, then small birds
Flitter out into the milky air.

Slowly things begin to connect,
School buses flicker along the berm,
Stitching together corners of fields
With houses, barns, patches of woods,
Things rise to take substance.

If I sold this house and land,
Took cash to the city and passed
Out hundred dollar bills all day
To destitute people, by evening
I could join them in the fog.

What I Know about Owls

They can break the night like glass.
They can hear a tick turn over
In the fur of a mouse thirty acres away.
Their eyes contain a tincture of magic
So potent they see cells dividing in
The hearts of their terrified victims.
You cannot hear their dismaying who,
You cannot speak their fearsome name
Without ice clattering in your arteries.

But in daytime owls rest in blindness,
Their liquids no longer boiling.
There is a legend that if you are careful
And foolishly ambitious, you can approach
Them and stroke for luck and life
The feathers on their foreheads,
Risking always that later on some
Quiet night when you least expect it
The owl, remembering your transgression,
Will slice into your lamplight like a razor,
Bring you down splayed from your easy chair,
Your ribcage pierced, organs raked
From their nests, and your head slowly
Rolling down its bloody pipe into
The fierce acids of its stomach.

A Romance for the Wild Turkey

They are so cowardly and stupid
Indians would not eat them
For fear of assuming their qualities.

The wild turkey always stays close
To home, flapping up into trees
If alarmed, then falling out again.
When shot it explodes like a balloon
Full of blood. It bathes by grinding
Itself in coarse dirt, is incapable
Of passion or anger, knows only
Vague innocence and extreme caution,
Walking around in underbrush
Like a cantilevered question mark,
Retreating at least hint of danger.

I hope when the wild turkey
Dreams at night it flies high up
In gladness under vast islands
Of mute starlight, its silhouette
Vivid in the full moon, guided always
By radiant configurations high
Over chittering fields of corn
And the trivial fires of men,
Never to land again nor be regarded
As fearful, stupid, and unsure.

The Brain of the Spider

Imagine a spider's brain,
The various colored segments of its matter:
Crimson for power, blue for balance,
Green for judgment, yellow for cunning.
Think how it inspires the shape of dew,
How it squares frost and causes
The silver sweep of its filaments
To stroke your face in woods and streets.
Regard the air it fixes between strands,
Its careful allowances for time and space.
Then consider what is most complex:
The unnerving grayness of its patience,
White speed of its sudden charges,
The raven segment it maintains for death.

But Bird

Some things you should forget,
But Bird was something to believe in.
Autumn '54, twenty, drafted,
Stationed near New York en route
To atomic tests in Nevada.
I taught myself to take
A train to Pennsylvania Station,
Walk up Seventh to 52d Street,
Looking for music and legends.
One night I found the one
I wanted. Bird.

Five months later no one was brave
When the numbers ran out.
All equal—privates and colonels—
Down on our knees in the slits
As the voice counted backward
In the dark turning to light.

But "Charlie Parker" it said
On the Birdland marquee,
And I dug for the cover charge,
Sat down in the cheap seats.
He slumped in from the kitchen,
Powder blue serge and suedes.
No jive Bird, he blew crisp and clean,
Bringing each face in the crowd
Gleaming to the bell of his horn.
No fluffing, no wavering,
But soaring like on my old
Verve waxes back in Ohio.

Months later, down in the sand,
The bones in our fingers were
Suddenly x-rayed by the flash.
We moaned together in light
That entered everything,
Tried to become the earth itself
As the shock rolled toward us.

But Bird. I sat through three sets,
Missed the last train out,
Had to bunk in a roach pad,
Sleep in my uniform, almost AWOL.
But Bird was giving it all away,
One of his last great gifts,
And I was there with my
Rosy cheeks and swan neck,
Looking for something to believe in.

When the trench caved in it felt
Like death, but we clawed out,
Walked beneath the roiling, brutal cloud
To see the flattened houses,
Sheep and pigs blasted,
Ravens and rabbits blind,
Scrabbling in the grit and yucca.

But Bird. Remember Bird.
Five months later he was dead,
While I was down on my knees,
Wretched with fear in
The cinders of the desert.

The Light

Warm evenings our house fills with light
And seeks breezes in its curtains.
I think of old, hot summer visits
With my uncle Joe, the miner from Indiana,
Blinking in his kitchen as he washed
A whole lightless day from his skin,
So weary he could barely change his shirt.
Yet when I begged he'd take his ball glove
Down from a peg in the closet and play catch,
Spinning a baseball with me in the alley
Until dinner, remembering tricks and
Fancy moves he'd learned pitching in
The Three-I League before his arm went sore
And they sent him home to the mines.

After dinner we'd rest with family
On the porch. Then Joe would rise
And beckon me to escort him
To the Moose Club. At the bar
His admirers tousled my hair
And set him up with round after round
Of Pabst as tribute to his best days.

One twilight as I followed him lurching
Home from the bar, a thin layer
Of ribbed clouds lit up and stretched
Across the sky past towers of cumulus.
As the sun slid away in a stripe
Of luminous pink, it silhouetted
The buildings of the little town.

Dazzled, I tried to detain him,
Wanting to share this glowing with him.
But he stopped only for a moment to gaze,
Wanting his bed, knowing that the numb
Moon spinning through clouds was all
The light he needed to find his way home.

Diz's Face

One of Diz's routines was to come on stage
And ask for the crowd's indulgence while
His group tuned up. Then he'd stomp
The floor and everybody'd hit one clinker.
"That's good enough for jazz," he'd say,
His great, wide face opening like a blossom
As he launched them into "Manteca."

Once in the '50s I went with friends
To hear his big band play a Cleveland club.
Between sets we spoke in awe of his flurries,
Powerful, cascading notes, amazing turns,
Notes perfectly formed, time locked in,
And the crazy, wriggle-hipped dancing.

Suddenly my friends looked past me in awe.
Tap-tap-tap-tap, on my shoulder—
When I turned there was Diz's face,
That marvelous, gleeful apple which could
Become a pear. He pointed down to my coat
Fallen from a chair to the floor,
Gave me a wink and went on to the bar.

Last year he toured our town.
Before he played he cautioned,
"Y'all remember, I'm 75 years old."
Then his cheeks ripened and he
Dazzled us with a few strong licks.

Now here is his buoyant face in the paper.
Gone easily as he slept, it says.

In sixty years I've spent maybe thirty hours
In the same room with Dizzy Gillespie.
But here's my crazy, board-legged boogie
For him who once touched my shoulder.
Having no rights at all in this matter,
I'll presume to say anyway, by God,
Diz, that was good enough for jazz.

Romance

This frightened, horny boy
Sits in a jazz club full of
Jungle ferns and leopard skins.

A piano trio is playing,
Dulcet and precise,
"My One and Only Love."

Hank Jones or Billy Taylor?
Al Haig? Ellis Larkins?
It does not matter.

What counts is this song
About something we do not even
Presume to hope for anymore.

Just in time, this wistful,
Tipsy boy hears about love
So sure it lasts a lifetime.

The Existential Year

I read the first three pages
  of the introduction to
    Being and Nothingness a dozen times.

I incessantly searched
  the streets for a woman
    who looked like Juliette Greco.

I learned to pronounce
  the word "Heidegger." I wore
    my coat on my shoulders

and long scarves which twisted
  agonizingly in the wind.
    I always looked

as if I were about
  to barf up my brains
    I vowed I would never

look backward or forward,
  knowing that Being
    was enough In-itself.

The Beautiful Ethiopian Navy

Having grown up far from the sea,
My friends didn't lightly heave-to
And go yo-ho-ho. They were men
Of the brush and distant peaks,
Young, reedy, black, intense,
They smoked unfiltered cigarettes
And drank straight rum.
Women turned to watch us pass,
Them in their crisp whites,
Me in my rumpled jacket and tie,
Negash, Maconan, Tassew, Seifu,
And Zimmer, like a rolling garden
Of dahlias and one elated lily.

Never have I had such friends again.
Brothers we declared ourselves,
Teaching songs to each other
And stories, how to throw spears
And footballs in Golden Gate Park,
Arguing games, books, religion
In the bars of San Francisco.

As I have remembered them,
Please do not tell me they are all
Likely gone, my beautiful fellows
From Asmara, Gondar, Harar, Diredawa,
Wandering parched lands of famine
And dying with the animals, or finished
In the bloody spray of politics.

Thirty years ago I watched them sail
Away to the other side of the world.
I have not had such friends again.

The Weathers of Love

1

Outdoors all day with you
In weather that cracks
Our small ear bones and drives
Rain through stones,
Snapping our coats like sails,
Suddenly in late afternoon
The scud is swallowed by blue.
Tiny flowers unwrap in sunlight,
Moss begins to passion.
So we have done it again,
Walked all day to love.

2

Today there was light sifting
Of snow from a joyless sky,
No great burden, just something
For us to bear up under.
But tonight we count on nothing.
The house begins cracking,
Big dogs moan on their rugs,
Pipes grow cold and indifferent,
Chill slips into our knuckles.
Twenty false steps outdoors
In the frigid, hard edges of air would
Shiver us, so we hold each other
And give the fire everything it needs.

3

You swat a sunlit cabbage moth
With your white baseball cap,
Shouting and flinging organic dust.

The garden goes on contending
With itself, great heads wrap and tighten,
Vines quietly pump up their fruits,
Vegetables sit on their secrets.

Still you imagine perfection
And fear the gnawing worm.
I cheer you on,
Get that son of a bitch!
I fall in love some more.

4

What to say to our children
Of our long time
In the weathers of love?

That it was never what we predicted,
But what we learned in time.

That to see you waving to me
From a hazy distance is as precious
As holding you in my arms.

That sometimes on a rainy day
Just knowing you are
In the next room saves my life.

A Rant against Losses

Word has come of my friend's death in London.
In my desolation memories begin to roll.
I recall once looking for him in the pubs
When a young barman, pondering my inquiry,
Smirked, "Red nose and a pint of cider, right?
The knobby one who zigzags when he walks?"

I should have slammed his pearly teeth,
Stood him on his diapered head and shaken
The little drums from his ears! Even now
It soothes me to hope that his old age
Becomes tawdry, that his hair falls out,
That his joints ignite and ache incessantly.

For my friend was worn fine with civility,
A wise, endearing man, lover of words,
To be respected beyond the capacity
Of any modish, indifferent, callow wag.
Goddamn ridiculous, vacant youth,
And piss on you, death, and fuck you!

Raw and Absolute

Grinding his ropy cheeks,
A pitcher bends forward
And peers at the signal,
Bobs his blue-eyed head,
Then twists extravagantly
Into a broad windup.

But with his arms swung back,
The shadow from his cap dims
His forehead, and his uniform
Slips like a locust shell.

He hides the ball on the nest
Of his crescent paunch.
When he cocks his arm to throw
It is creaky and windblown.

He comes around as if half
Asleep, spittle stringing from
His open mouth. When he releases
He almost topples. The ball
Grows wings and flaps away.

When it comes back from
The catcher he rolls it
In his liver-spotted claw
And mumbles threats at it,
Pretending not to see the manager
Striding slowly toward the mound.

The Seed Bearers

I dream the Spring of 1901,
My grandfathers walk together in
Their shirt sleeves through woods,
Trailing smoke from their cigars.
The French and the German man,
A miner and accountant,
Never met so far as I know,
But talking American,
They laugh and josh each other
Like colors plucked randomly
From light and clouds, nurtured
In dim pods, then bloomed forth
Arm-in-arm in springtime.

Victoria has died, Bismarck, and Verdi.
Hemingway, Ellington, Lorca are born.
We've fought a pitiless Civil War.
McKinley has been re-elected
And soon will be assassinated.
We have been rudely led for years,
Assaulted by our inventions,
But my grandfathers walk on,
Guileless and blossoming in America.

*   *   *

Now the century has almost passed,
We approach the double millennium.
My grandfathers are long dead,
But my son, his son, and I,

Still colors plucked from light
And clouds, stroll in the spring.
Many great people have died.
We do not know who has just
Been born. The vacant wars have
Gone on, a president gunned down,
Another resigned, we are spent out,
Having been cruelly led for years.
But this is what we can do,
Grandfather, father, and son,
We blossom forth arm-in-arm
Through spring trees and grasses,
Burrs and seed fluff clinging
To our jeans and t-shirts, strolling,
Talking together in the last light
Of this old and failed century.

Another Place

You come to a place in winter woods
That seems remembered, a foundation
Full of rusty tools, door knobs, dog bones,
Peach stones, scissors, where hard winds
Blew for years through blackened timbers.
Small wings of frost still strive on weeds,
But so many things are missing now,
Pervasive regret has assumed the place.
You feel fine snow flitter down
And settle into the ancient residue,
Gathering in cockleburs, ear holes,
Joints of aspen, sockets of your eyes.
Slowly it begins to change you
Into something better than yourself.

Big Blue Train

The big blue train coughs,
coughs again and is silent,
then resolves itself and slams
its pistons down once more.

They stroke three times, sighing
and blowing, then stagger cold.
Next time they bluster once,
hold the cycle and gather fire.

Fire on fire, and the engine
heats up glowing on the tracks.
It hisses, tensing its wheel rods,
impatient to connect its gears.

Clouds of steam and black smoke
billow up to the station canopy,
slip along the filthy girders
to curtain out to the sky.

Zimmer pulls the whistle cord
and cleaves the chill air in two.
Doors are slamming, signals flash,
people kiss on the concourse.

He taps the gritty meters,
eases slowly up on the brake
and brings the throttle down—
the engine knocks and heaves.

A long, echoing chain of thunder,
then the big blue train inches
forward out of the station,
creaking and swinging its lanterns,

slides into the early dawn,
through lighted grids of the city,
faces in its windows growing
vague in the rising light.

New Poems

Entrance to the Sky

I

He stared in a window
through reflections of a drifting sky
at a still life on a table—
an assortment of things,
pastel bowls and saucers,
a serene spill of fruit
out of oval shadows
into a patch of sunlight.
It was an image he might
have held forever.

But because the movement of sky
made him restless, he walked
off into the broad landscape and saw
a redwinged blackbird whirl
in bright wind with a hawk,
shrieking and spearing with
its beak again and again
until hawk turned its razor head
and rasped a single warning.
Blackbird turned and flapped away.

He remembers wanting to rise
and retreat with the blackbird,
to help it bear its losses
slowly under the sky
over the delicate spill
of fields and greening woods.

2

The time the sky was interrupted,
the day moon bit the sun at noon.
Light bled down from yellow, orange to tan.
This was not the world he lived in.

Birds huddled and mewled together,
flowers swiveled aimlessly in half glow,
every dog in the township started to bark
as chill crawled up his legs
along his back and into his hair.

3

One night, the year of the troubled sky,
he saw bright hearts of clouds explode
along the horizon, rumbling as light
snapped from billow to boiling.
But over his head swept the milky way
shot through by streaks of falling stars—
it was a night so full of contrasts and signals
unraveling in gentle breezes over the trees,
he thought it meant the storms had ended.
Yet later these clouds drew overhead and wind
stopped sibilating in branches to drive another
deluge across the beleaguered landscape.
It rained so hard the stars fell out of the sky.
At morning, darkness, held down at corners
by rivers and lakes, again would not withdraw.

4

He doesn't recall what happened
after it was established
they would remove the lump
and the operation was set
for the following morning.
He remembers only a desire
to be out under the sky.

Next thing, he is sitting
on the fender of his pick-up
in a supermarket lot.
He is eating a large,
perfect, yellow apple.
People avoid him as
they pass into the store—
this strange, gray man
in rumpled shirt and tie,
munching and looking up
at light and passing clouds.

5

Summertime up on this ridge
the sky takes more than half his life.
Mornings even before daybreak,
birds start piping the air's intentions.
Mist shrugs loose from the brush,
crawls up hillsides into rays of light.

Fields are cut and in stubble,
round bales steam in the afternoon sun
amidst flurries of larks and bobolinks
ransacking clouds for their ruined nests.

There is the slow resplendence of sunset,
then stars begin their silent stitching,
turning in massive, circular pathways.

From time to time an irregular light
bores slowly through the powdery tracks,
bending sudden, impossible angles,
growing dim, then brilliant
as if it might descend
to visit his small circle of fire.

He has faith in whatever the sky brings—
rain, heat, snow, ice, dark.
He believes in morning, noon, and night,
in sunrise, sunset, and midnight.
Even these small, unnerving lights
might bring down to his life
some sudden, lustrous conclusion.

6

Everything is turning white:
Hands, hair, ears, eyes, and brain.
He's passed through days and years.
Now colors are drained from his seasons.
Except in late summer—there is
the color of chicory to love,
bluer than rocking chops of water,
than buntings swinging on timothy,
or veins on the backs of his hands.

When the end comes
he will assume this azure—
and because he has loved
the blue of chicory,
because he has taken on
the color of the heavens,
he will be permitted
entrance to the sky.

The Books

*"The printed word is part of a vestigial order
we are moving away from."*—Sven Birkerts

The first time you opened one—
Pages winging lightly as you turned,
Making delicate, puffing scrolls
Of air, aroma of paper
And ink feathering your nostrils—
You knew the rest of your life
Would be part of their singular flights,
Vast flocks, brave migrations.

Now recall their variety.
Fragile volumes fanning at cusps
Of flowers. Tomes bursting
Out of meadows when alarmed.
Earth books, star books, sea books,
Some that mutter to themselves,
Scratching earnestly for seeds,
Others that clang and strike like
Thunderbolts out of the sky's core—
Yet such forlorn creatures in the end,
Hunched over, swaying back and forth,
With light seeping out of their eyes.
They disappear like ancient magic,
Like phantoms of lost animals
Or ghosts of chestnuts and elms.

Some evening years from now
You might think you hear them rustling
In shadowy branches, their small songs

Rising out of your dusky dreams,
But then the silence will descend
And you will realize once more
That they have gone away forever
Before you even thought to say goodbye.

Here is my last great privilege,
to be regarded by eyes that
devote themselves to idolatry.
I shall never expect anything
better than to stand like the sun
amidst this polychrome ardor
with bees nuzzling my cuffs,
still believing I can grow roots.

Love Poem

1

Last days before first frost
we stroll out hand in hand
to see yellow sulfurs lift
in multitudes
over the fields
flittering in ecstatic pairs
to descend
and spangle the hay

2

Months later
trudging winter fields
in the morning sun
we see their million
rapturous spirits have risen
through layers of drift
to glitter
on the snow crust

Grouse

I mention once to our neighbor
That we've never tasted grouse.
One day he comes to the door
And puts a dead bird in my hands.
"But what do I do with it?" I ask.

"Stand on the wings and pull steady
On the claws," and then he leaves.

So I take this frail corpse outside
In the cold and, yes, I spread the wings,
And, yes, stand on them, holding hands
With the fallen angel, pulling steadily,
Ripping it apart.

What comes off are backbone and head
In my hands, what's left in bloody snow
Are its sweet breast and wings,
Which I clean of feathers and skin
And hold in the palm of my hand,
A ball of delicate meat the size
Of a small, green apple.

Before the Moon Came Up Last Night

We walked on the old road
That is crossed by the milky way.
Suddenly the hill's silhouette
Erupted in squawling and growls,
A swirl of deadly encounter
Raging on and on and on,
Until it faded into
The dimming trees.

This morning we found remains
Of slaughter: drifting turkey feathers,
Frantic scribbles of retreat,
Blood drops burning in old snow.

Tonight at dusk coyotes sing
Back and forth from woods
To woods—folk songs of triumph
And sweetness, perhaps,
Or ancient Serbian melodies.
Here I am, they say, there you are,
We've slept well and made love,
Now we must hunt again.

I imagine them tugging
The sunset back and forth,
Eyes crimson with happiness,
Tongues lolling out of their mouths,
Heads thrown back so far
If you were the moon,
You could look straight down
The shafts of their throats
To see the proud, glowing hearts.

Divestment

For weeks as I worked I listened
To mice bustling in the garage walls,
But one day an alien silence clutched the air.

As I strained to cast off books, records,
Forsaken manuscripts, dusty residue of years,
I felt a long line of cells pull apart along
My chest and abdomen into my groin.

Later I found a reason behind the wheelbarrow
—a rope of limpid pebbles—
The abandoned six-foot skin of a bull snake.

The Poetry of Aging Men

Avoiding shadows of heavy clouds,
The drone wasp on the bench outside
My window grinds the brain of a cricket
With its mandibles while spreading
Its wings to dry in autumn sun.

Abruptly it zips off out of sight
To make some ghastly pinch and slash.
When I look again it is back in place,
Revolving the aspects of its eyes.

All summer it has done its duties,
Looping through the windowlight
To hunt food for the larvae,
In spare time daubing round
The nest that hangs from the eave.

Now groggy in the fading warmth,
It goes on with its vacuous work.
Soon enough the last place where
It lights will become a grave,
The vacant chambers of the nest
Will cup ill winds and tremble
Before crumbling onto the snow crust.

Greatness

I no longer court disillusionment,
Think about greatness less and less.
The only history worth cherishing
Is recorded in annual rings of trees,
The thickest ones recalling years
Of perfect rain feathering down
Between intervals of clouds and light—
Years when eyes of animals are full and serene
And birds linger until November before
Massing to lift in huge flocks of reluctance,
Circle once, tip their wings to ancient verities,
Then string away to silence and the year's conclusion.

Milkweed

1

The old pod of Eli's face splits open
And speaks, sludge in ditches
At the corners of his mouth and eyes,
Twigs hanging from his robe sleeves.

He tells me, "Know where the cow pond
Used to be? Where they bulldozed?
The fence was just above there,
Beside where we laid that drain pipe.

It run down below the draw
Where a hickory fell on the shed.
Me and Lester drove a stake there
In the snow, Christmas of '45,
When we come back from the army.

No, we didn't have no survey done,
But we shook hands on that corner.
It's there, by God—and it counts.
You tell 'em Eli says so!"

2

I remember years before we were laying
Drain pipe along the field road,
A boulder dropped loose and blustered
Down the ditch. We came spraying out
Like a bunch of grasshoppers
Until it finally wedged to a stop.

When we finished jittering
We saw it was going to take
At least four normal men
To horse that baby out.

But young Eli jumped down,
Strapped on and sailed it out
Of the bottom like milkweed fluff.

We shook our heads in wonder.
We thanked God for young Eli,
A man who could show us what
Was possible in this world.

The Name for Money

Romanian refugee children came
To our block when I was nine,
A nervous brother and sister
In bright, strange clothes.
When I tried to speak to them
They held hands and peered at me
The way my deaf Aunt Mame did.

The only Romanian word I could
Find in our home dictionary
Was the name for money.
"Leu," I said to them, "leu,"
Showing a nickel in my palm.

I did not understand sadness,
Had never been lost. I remember
The girl reached out to touch
My hand as if her arm
Were a thousand miles long.

The Example

The papers on my desk out of hand,
Rampant as an unkempt lilac bush,
I think of Leonard the obscure,
A memory from an ancient summer job,
A soiled man, teeth rotten to the gums,
With hair like gray, electric shock.
He lived by his wits and last strength
In a wretched shack down by the tracks,
A man without wife, family, or language
We could understand, his smile abiding
As he sat apart from us in the truck bed.

We'd drop him off with pruners, saw,
Jug of water, and bag of day-old bread
At the biggest clumps of unkempt bushes
In the parks. At day's end when we picked
Him up, he'd be sitting on the ground smoking
His broken, taped-up pipe, the bush subdued,
Trimmed to cane, tied in neat stacks
Ready for hauling. He'd pull himself wearily
Over the tailgate and sit downwind from
Our teenage wisecracks. Secretly I thought
He was amazing. Even now as I remember him,
My fingers begin riffling through stacks
Of inventories, letters, queries, reports,
Once more I lower my wild, gray head,
Smile my abiding smile and work and work.

Suck It Up

Two pugs on the undercard step through
The ropes in satin robes,
Pink Adidas with tassels,
Winking at the women in the crowd.
At instructions they stare down hard
And refuse to touch their gloves,
Trying to make everyone believe
That this will be a serious dust-up.

But when the bell rings they start
Slapping like a couple of Barbie Dolls.
One throws a half-hearted hook,
The other flicks out his jab,
They bounce around for a while
Then grab each other for a tango.
The crowd gets tired of booing
And half of them go out for beer,
But I've got no place to hide.

A week after a cancer scare,
A year from a detached retina,
Asthmatic, overweight, trickling,
Drooling, bent like a blighted elm
In my pajamas and slippers,
I have tuned up my hearing aids to sit in
Numbness without expectation before
These televised Tuesday Night Fights.

With a minute left in the fourth,
Scuffling, they butt their heads
By accident. In midst of all the catcalls

And hubbub suddenly they realize
How much they hate each other.
They start hammering and growling,
Really dealing, whistling combinations,
Hitting on the breaks and thumbing.
At last one guy crosses a stiff jab
With a roundhouse right and the other
Loses his starch. The guy wades into
The wounded one, pounding him
Back and forth until he goes down,
Bouncing his head hard on the canvas.

The count begins but he is saved
By the bell and his trainers haul
Him to his stool as the lens zooms in.

I come to the edge of my La-Z-Boy,
Blinking and groaning from my incision,
Eager for wise, insightful instruction.

He gets a bucket of water in his face,
A sniff on the salts while the cutman
Tries to close his wounds with glue.
His nose is broken, eyes are crossed,
His lips bleed like two rare steaks.
His cornermen take turns slapping his cheeks.
"Suck it up!" they shout.
"Suck it up!"

Dear Mom

At last I am able to tell you it was I
Who started the Great Blizzard of 1940.
Do you remember? It was a washday.
I helped you shave soap from bars
And sprinkle it into hot, gray water.
We stirred and rinsed the clothes,
And as I turned the wringer crank
In heavy steam I made a wish.

Suddenly soap chips spiraled up
And swirled to grim clouds in the sky.
Snow came as fleecy powdering
Then began to split and multiply,
Driving down hard across our town
To mount deep, benumbing drifts
In the streets and over houses.

I remember you struggling with baskets
Of frozen laundry in the yard,
Your housedress flapping, face blue
And pinched with the awful chill.

The storm had come a long way
To make us feel small,
Our house trembled in its clutches
As light drained out of the windows.
I remember poor Dad frightened,
Weary, struggling home at last
In darkness out of the snow blasts.

I regret my rashness and stupidity,
But I was a child, afraid and stunned
By what I had caused. It's taken me
More than fifty years to confess.
Now it is too late. But even at this
Impossible hour, I beg your forgiveness.

Passage

Years ago, walking home from classes,
I came upon an old black couple
hunched down on the sidewalk over
the mangled corpse of their dog.

The woman swayed above the body,
her shoulders quaking with misery,
the man had his hand on her back.

I stood in silence beside their grief,
looking down at his worn jacket,
her sweater spattered with blood.

Finally, because I had no experience,
I imagined that words might serve,
"You'll have to get her another dog."

For a long time I listened to the throb
of her weeping, to traffic
sucking wind in the oily street.
My bones grew brittle as I waited.

At last the man drew his answer
heavily up from the deep, "That's all right.
You go on along," he said. "It's our sadness."

And Then I Drove On

Tunneling under ponderous levels
Of a winter storm, young and imperishable,
On my way to see Suzanne in Pittsburgh,
I run my old Chevy through a long burrow
Of freezing shadow and light, lit up by love
And riffs of jazz to fling the drifts aside.
Then I begin a slide and twirl that still
Makes my chest echo when I think of it,
A furious spin across the turnpike median,
Three times around, almost rolling
On the last, finally coming to rest
Wrong way in the opposite lane,
Engine dead, me whimpering,
But somehow still with wits enough
To turn the key and start it up again,
Easing onto the shoulder just seconds
Before a semi whomps past through
The driving snow, its airhorn blaring.

Blood Lock

Operation Desert Rock, 1955

Amongst all the stalwart words we'd been fed
By officers and physicists about making history
And doing our duty, why do I remember only
What Sergeant Pipko said, just before countdown
To the Turk shot?
                              As we cowered like victims
In the trenches, a breeze shifted above the aurora.
Some magpies fussed in brittlebush
And air was tense across the blasted yucca flats.
Pipko's words seemed like such pathetic things,
Appeared to make no sense at all, yet in his terror,
I know now he was trying to put some name
On this unspeakable thing, trying to do his job
And give us courage—but his voice strained,
Scrabbling like a bare branch over stone.

He told us about blood lock. How his father used
To warn him about something called blood lock.
How they kept fifty pigs on their farm in Missouri,
And when slaughter time came, they would run
Them into the yard, where he and his brother
Chased them down and dragged them to the father,
Who'd pull a knife across their throats.

"Pig can scream even when its pipe is slit," he croaked.
"They fall down in their own blood and roll themselves
  Like they's tryin' to get it back inside their skins.
  There'd be half a dozen still twitchin' around
  Before we'd cinch them up on the frame to bleed.

Then my ol' man'd make us stop for a while.
We'd go in the barn and drink well water,
Sit together for a spell in the cool.
Blood lock, he warns us.
You boys best remember this.
It can turn your soul to red.
It's a thing that,
If it ever gets ahold of you,
Makes you want to go on killin' forever."

Pearl-Handled Pistols

1

Barney sat down at our table in The Palms.
He'd been drinking and hurting for weeks,
Misery spilled out of his eyes and mouth.
His wife had left him for another man.
Barney said, "He comes in here tonight—
I got something for him," and he flashed
The inside pocket of his sport coat.
The blood drained out of my head
When I saw the pearl-handled pistol.

My God—we were so young,
We didn't know what else to do!
So we sat there drinking beer with
That furious, suffering, forsaken man,
Who was ready to do bloody murder.

2

The pearl-handled pistol nested among
Rolled-up socks in a dresser drawer,
Like a maggot in the heart of our house.
My father showed it to me once,
Then where he kept the bullets
In his closet. It seemed comforting
To me, right as a glass of milk,
Ready as a household tool—
Hammer in the tool chest
Or tire jack in the trunk.
But he warned, "This is no toy."

Of course, next time I was alone
In the house, the first thing I did
Was to get it out and practice
Quick draws in front of a mirror.
But when I looked for the bullets,
He'd moved them to another place.
I felt the worm crawl up a vein
Into my heart and grind
The shame into my chambers.

As I Walked the Road

trees made a sound
  like brushed drums
    begging a dance,
coaxing the clouds
  to bring down
    ponderous rain.
Long lanes opened
  from the sky,
    and spillways
down the leaves.

  Sudden as a dragonfly
    lightning slashed
across the road,
  shivered a maple
    just yards ahead
of where I walked.
  Storm clouds plunged
    on over foothills
as if this
  had never occurred.

  But the tree
was on fire
  and smoke tangled
    in crosswinds
through ragged veins
  at the backs
    of my eyes.

The End before the End

My friend is driving me from Denver
To Colorado Springs the long way
On the scenic route, when his car
Vapor-locks and lurches to the berm.

Two rickety, old pals—there we are,
Many decades past our undaunted youths,
One diabetic, the other asthmatic,
Fifty miles from insulin or ventolin,
In a dead car, with shadows lengthening
And strong wind rising with our stress.

As we walk we contemplate
The vast, chilled foothills of age,
Envision snow descending with the light
To bury the road and blind us,
So that we waver off into aspens
To die, our bones found in spring,
Unglued like ancient furniture,
Scattered and whittled by animals—
Pitiful, old fools, stunned by years,
Paying at last for early excesses
And now for final misjudgments.

for John McGowan

In Apple Country

A year begins with marriage in apple country,
Immaculate drift of lace in light crosswinds,
Consummation of dusts, caverns of blossoms,
Endless circles forming and expanding.

As a child I drew circles for hours,
Arcing the compass around its point
To feel the pleasure of circumference,
Roundness conjoined, swallowing, embracing,
Shoebox full of buckeyes in their husks,
Baseballs, acorns, bags of marbles,
Tulip bulbs, yo-yo's, dandelions—
But ripe apples sliced across always
Made the most perfect circles of all.

Late in harvest good pickers wear gloves
To keep their fingertips from frostbite,
The delicate twist and pluck—
A hundred and fifty bushels a day.

Do apples die when they are picked?
When they tumble from baskets and bags,
Bruised, crushed, slithering under bootsoles?
When the first bite is taken,
Sweet death dribbling onto the chin?

In truth they triumph and abide.
If all the apples ripening
On one fall day and all the circles
Ever grown in these orchards
Draped across the driftless hills,

Were counted by a great master,
They would total the number of stars
In western skies on an autumn night.

I lean back in my garden chair and watch
The great harvests turn slowly in vast distances—
Red, yellow, green, their blemishes and tiny wormholes
Revolving in the October sky all the way
Out to the round ends of the universe.